The Ugly Toad

By Jenny Mernickle

Illustrations by Matthew Hanisch

To my husband Gord and our children
Calvin, Tessa, and Gordon Jr.

You inspire me to follow my dreams. I will love you
forever, and you will always be in my heart.

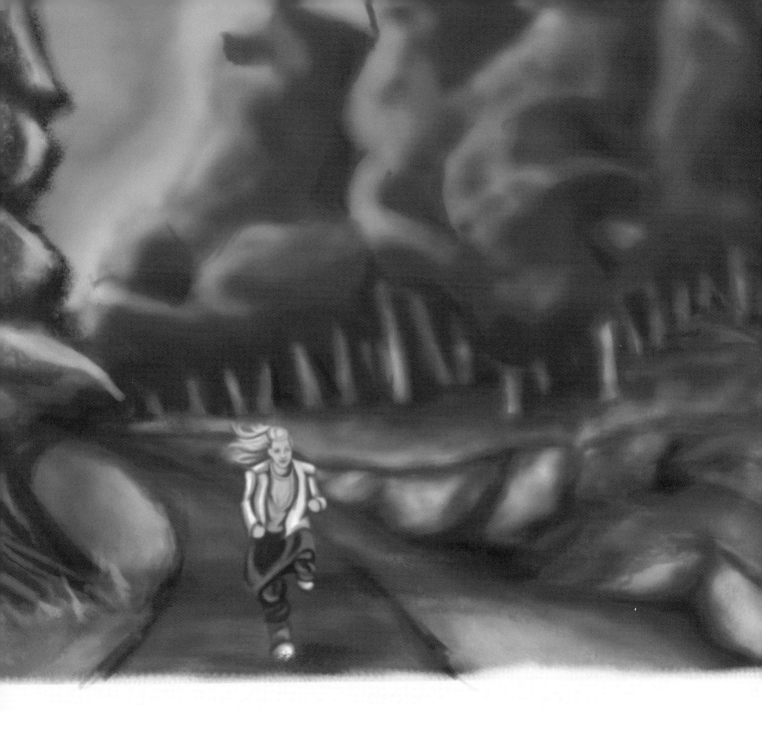

Happy little Tessa skipped down the road

Stopped by the water, saw an ugly Toad.
"What an ugly thing to make," she thought.
She couldn't understand it, even for the creature's sake.

"Why are you so ugly?" she simply asked of him.
"Oh silly girl," Toad said, lifting his tiny chin.
"Isn't it so funny, too odd to be true. I was sitting here thinking that very thing about you!"

"You're a funny little girl
with all that yellow hair.

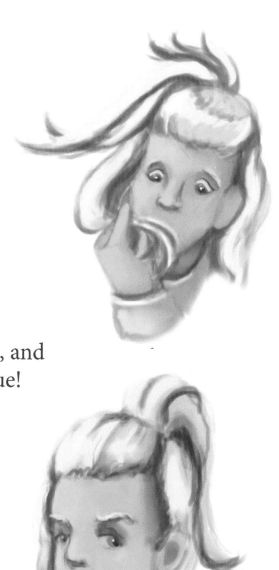

Look at your nose, and
that short tongue!

Couldn't catch a fly,
not a single one."

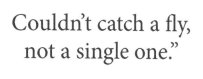

"Oh my, Sir Toad, I won't catch flies. Why would I...why, why, why?
You really don't see well with those big bug eyes.
I'm pretty! Daddy says it's true. Daddy says I don't look anything like you."

The Toad just smiled. "I can see very well. If you weren't so close to the sky,
you could tell. You are so very tall. I see no point to that at all."

"Silly Toad, you're really odd. You must have fallen off your log. I'm pretty Daddy says so! And I can walk and run. You're just a Toad, you can't have fun."

Toad just croaked, "You are the one who cannot see. Did your brain flip while you hung from that tree?"

"I hop, I swim and float, little girl, and that is no joke.

Ask the fish in the pond, they've seen me play. They wish they were me… or so they say!"

"Why is the Toad so glad? When people pick on me, I get really mad. Why doesn't he hop off when I poke fun at him? That's what I do when I feel grim. This talking Toad hasn't moved an inch. I said mean things, and he didn't even flinch."

"I'm going to ask him, that's what I'll do. –Hey Sir Toad, what is up with you?

Why aren't you mad, and crying boo hoo? If people called me names, that's what I would do.

Sometimes I get sad, and mad, and so upset. What part of me insulting you don't you get?"

"Silly girl, you missed a part. Listen up, and let it pierce your heart. This is a truth that will ease your pain. If you listen now, you will never be the same. People pass me by each and every day. They say the same mean things along the way."

"When I was little, I used to hop away and cry, but then my Mommy said something very sly. People have opinions, and say things that are cruel. But what Mommy said, now that was totally cool."

Tessa got impatient and began to shout.
"Tell me Toad, for goodness sake! Can't you see my life's at stake? Croak it out, I won't get mad. Maybe it will help, and I won't be so sad."

"Alright," he said. "Here it is…a clue. It changed my life, and it can change yours, too."

The Toad sat up, and raised his head. He looked right at Tessa, and here's what he said:

"You told me I was ugly, and others have, too. But my Mommy says…"

"IT'S ONLY TRUE... IF I BELIEVE YOU."

The End.

The inspiration for *The Ugly Toad* came
from the following Scriptures:

"As a man thinks in his heart, so he is."
Proverbs 23:7

"Then you will know the truth,
and the truth will set you free."
John 8:32

Teacher's Guide:

The Scriptures provide teachers and parents with an excellent tool that they can use to help young children explore their own minds and thought processes. They can also help guide children to:

- Create their own moral compasses

- Learn how to interact with others, and approach them with respect and kindness

- Build self-esteem, and a sense of self-worth

- Give them tools to use against bullies

- Help them understand the importance of self-love

The Story of *The Ugly Toad*

The Ugly Toad is based on the following Scriptures:

"As a man thinks in his heart, so he is."
Proverbs 23:7

"Then you will know the truth, and the truth will set you free."
John 8:32

In other words:
What you choose to think about and dwell on in this life will help determine what type of person you will be. Understanding this simple premise can set you free from self-doubt and self-denigration; it will allow you to live a happy and satisfied life.

Questions for Children

1. How did the story of *The Ugly Toad* make you feel? Sad? Mad? Why?

2. Do you think it was right for Tessa to talk to the Toad that way?

3. Did you feel sorry for Tessa, the Toad, or both? Why?

4. When someone says something mean to you, what do you do?

5. How does it make you feel? Why?

6. When someone says something mean, do you tell someone, or keep it to yourself? Who do you tell?

7. How does telling make you feel?

8. What lesson was the Toad trying to teach Tessa?

9. After reading *The Ugly Toad*, what did you learn?

10. What can bullies learn from reading *The Ugly Toad*?

About the Author

Jenny Mernickle is a writer, speaker, pastoral counselor, and President of the International Humanitarian Society. She has her Master's degree in Divinity, and loves to help people of all ages find their way to emotional health.

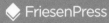 FriesenPress

Suite 300 - 990 Fort St
Victoria, BC, Canada, V8V 3K2
www.friesenpress.com

ISBN
978-1-4602-7558-0 (Paperback)
978-1-4602-7559-7 (eBook)

1. BISAC Code Education, Decision-Making & Problem Solving

Distributed to the trade by The Ingram Book Company

CPSIA information can be obtained at www.ICGtesting.com
Printed in the USA
LVIW01n2322111215
466380LV00005B/10